The Joy of Poems

Inspiring Poetry

ANGEL M. JIMENEZ

The Joy of Poems
INSPIRING POETRY

iUniverse books may be ordered through booksellers or by contacting:

iUniverse
1663 Liberty Drive
Bloomington, IN 47403
www.iuniverse.com
1-800-Authors (1-800-288-4677)

ISBN: 978-1-5320-2976-9 (sc)
ISBN: 978-1-5320-2978-3 (e)
ISBN: 978-1-5320-2977-6 (hc)

Library of Congress Control Number: 2017912141

Print information available on the last page.

iUniverse rev. date: 11/30/2017

To my wife Sonia

Our children

Nerlyne, Kaysie, and Angelson

&

Grandchildren

Arjan, Jayden, Alize, Scarlett, and Antonio

Trusting that each one follows his or her heart

Contents

Introduction

The most natural emotion in a person is the feeling of love. It just appears. It is there within us. It is accompanied by peace and happiness. This is ground zero. It is the origin and point of departure to begin and continue any other relationship in life. Of all the emotions, love is the most important and essential. As a matter of fact, any other action in life, whether we are aware or not, takes us back to ground zero. When it comes to love, we decorate the spheres of space, subjects, and objects with exotic romantic dimension to enhance the outlook and context of life, and poetry comes alive. Since the labyrinth of the mind likes to be challenged, *The Joy of Poems* tries to make a simplistic contribution to the wonderful world of poetic semantics with variations of colorful expressions. Let the mind freely dissolve into the reading, and rest upon your innate sources to enjoy the poems.

Out of many subjects covered in this book, I just elaborated above over the subject of love. The various subjects include poems of love, romanticism, friendship, inspiration, nature, encouragement, and other miscellaneous poems. If you have not yet scanned the table of contents, please check it out to get a flavor of the various titles. If these poems bring you relaxation and enjoyment, that is the greatest compliment to me.

Prologue

The poetry enthusiasts who usually read poems in silence should try to read poems aloud. You will discover a new delight with the rhythm and the sound of your voice. Imagine if written songs were handed to people to read silently while someone else played the music. Without a singer to voice the words, songs wouldn't have the same attraction. The same theory applies to poetry. Challenge yourself to read poetry aloud, emphasizing the words as the punctuation indicates. You will experience a higher degree of enjoyment as you hear the resounding echoes of the rhythm in your mind.

Love Poems

Finesse

The flair of your finesse is in the air.
Let's take a walk in the white sandy beach.
Forgive me if I look at you too much and sometimes stare.
My concentration could be intensive and gets out of reach.
I feel in the air energy of kisses and not as a figure of speech.

I want to get to know you as we caress this refined sand
And have a back-and-forth conversation
In this beautiful day and shining sun,
As the waves of water bounce, reflecting our actions,
And as people enjoy the beach's sensation.

Imagine how much of life together we can encompass.
This scenery will remain with us an entire life
With the rejoicing of folks crisscrossing in front of us,
Like children enjoying themselves that just arrived
From a tough winter and are now in a paradise.

Your voice rooted with your singular tone
Evokes my attention to reminisce.
Your conversation sounds like a compilation of poems
Desiring the rejoicing sound to be accompanied by a kiss,
To continue evermore in this total bliss.

Always in Love

The moon is falling in love with the night,
And so am I with my wife.
The moon has always been in love with the night and aroused,
And I have been the same with my spouse.

The sun descends through the mountain's view and the tree lines
To settle down the light for love in the night to realign,
Allowing the moon to rise,
To subtly set up the scenery to harmonize.

Let the night bring passions to the entire house.
By the touch of your hands, let the thrilling espouse.
Let the prettiest memories emanate harmonies with trust
And the lesser ones to settle into dust.

Look into my eyes and read the essence of my destiny enhanced.
I want to be entwined always in your presence.
Let's humbly increase the stage of hope and insurmountable love rising,
To continually throw chips into the fire to keep love and life sparkling.

Confession

The poem I yearn to devote to your existence
Is in my mind, demanding to be in black and white.
I feel it deeply in the internal of my unconscious,
And it does not wish to stay another moment in absence.
My hand trembles for assisting its scripture.
I can no longer conceal this adventure.
I relinquish, retaining to myself the poem of my life
Since her image lives in me daily.
I'm proud to reveal to the world my delight,
To express the divine passion that exists in me, lady!

Consent

Thank you for the invitation to your party and your courtesy.
The charisma of your voice is charming and zesty.
The sensitive look in your face endows me to look into your receptive eyes
And set out deeper into your soul, which reveals modesty under the sky.

Grant me with humbleness to be your gardener for more than hours.
For you to enjoy unique designs of plants and flowers.
Grown out of earth with the full power of nature to serve.
To enjoy everything in life as you deserve.

The flowers will be planted with love and dedication.
Maintained with the elements that are essentials
To precisely allow nature,
To maximize its fruition and culmination.

The garden will be an illustration of your personality,
A beautiful mirror image of your character and serenity.
You possess everything needed to be whole and happy.
I would just like to complement your diary!

Dreaming of You

The night that I dream of you, I will reveal everything unsaid.
Will be the night that I fall with the forces of nature into bed.
The dream will take me away into the night forever at last.
It will be a life span of an entire night together to makeup.
To live in happiness the two of us.
Until the ending life when I wake up.

It does not matter. We may share as best friends,
Although I prefer you to become my girlfriend.
I want to inspire your life
And have the charisma to convert you to my dear wife.
"Yes, dream my children," say mothers, fathers, the experienced and the wise.
One must persist and have big dreams all the time, as advised.
I will follow the guidance as birthrights.
The dreams will exist in days and nights.

The Jewel of Earth

The jewel that inspires.
The brilliance inside—one admires!
It's awakening when one finds it.
It is planted into the nest and grows as a flower.
Its color is bountiful and neutral because it is too beautiful.
Every person has different eyes to define its wonder
And deeply commits to searching every angle to discover the treasure.
If misplaced, one goes to the end of the universe to recuperate.

With conviction, it is the male,
Admiring the marvel jewel of earth called *female*!

Love's Symmetry

As a surrounding mass of water transfigures mountains in symmetrical sceneries,

That's the balance your presence instills in my life.

Everything looks so equivalent and perfect.

That is the inspiration of love.

The potential it carries.

The hope it inspires.

It is pure love.

Just love.

Love.

You

&

I

:

I

&

You

Love.

Just love.

It is pure love.

The hope it inspires.

The potential it carries.

That is the inspiration of love.

Everything looks so equivalent and perfect.

That's the balance your presence instills in my life.

As a surrounding mass of water transfigure mountains in symmetrical sceneries.

Marriage

Are you ready to commit, to fly high as a pair of white doves?
If you are self-centered, you are not apt to share love.
If the best you can offer is just for yourself,
You will be better off alone, not with someone else.

In order to immensely receive,
You have to with selflessness give.
To harvest and share the gift of love,
You must be willing to give it all.

To receive, you must first give.
It's the same as planting a vegetable seed.
At first, nothing is perceived.
You plant it.
You visit it.
You clean it.
You water it.
At the proper time to harvest,
You get compensated for the dedication harnessed.
The same attention that would bring you to be
The selfless person ready for happiness and bliss.

My Heart Beats Your Sound

The rhythm of my heart tells me you are my lady.
It sounds like a guitar with the sound of hearts on fire,
Pouring feelings for you daily
With profound sentiments and boiling desires.

Listen to the beats of my heart
Reverberating sounds of encounter,
Responding only to the tunes of your art
With resounding tones of power.

Let the hearts have a conversation of love
While we just look into our eyes,
Allowing our visions to disperse into our souls
With freedom advocated by the flight of doves into the open sky.

Occasional tears express the sentiments transcending our love.
Please put your face close to my cheekbones
Without boundaries thereof
To combine our tears so they won't run or dry alone!

My Love

Enthrall me in the servitude of your life forever.
It will be with pleasure to serve you whenever.
I shall conquer your heart with my natural zeal
Without remorse to your taste or to your passionate appeal.

I persist through time without rest,
Until you encounter the moment of your picturesque
To appease the beats of your heart,
Till you subside and tune yours to mine.

Together

I miss you every moment, day and night,
Imagining having you by my side
Walking in a pool of water leveled to my heart,
Feeling my emotions so light,
Encouraged by the imagination of your sight.

Why do I feel your presence so real?
The altered palpitation in my heart is not surreal.
I see the reflection of you as the water waves and glides.
How can you be here with me, being afar?
Why you have such intensive passion in your eyes?

When are we going to be close by?
Let it happen, God!
Vanish the space between me and her.
Let me have expectation.
Let life do its magic with the forces of nature.

Slow down. Relax, please!
I wholeheartedly want to make you feel at peace.
Nothing will satisfy me more than your happiness,
Reflected in your daily life
For us to enjoy side by side.

The Woman You Love

The woman you love should be upheld.
She puts on the line her entire life,
Carries on her shoulders the household.
Bears from her intimacy other lives.
Gives so much more than expected.
And pledges with tenderness, "The children are loved and protected."

A man who has not experienced the sacrifice at all
Of observing the bearing of his children
Is not a man in whole.
He missed the act of childbirth then.
And how his continuity of life gave the first cry
Or when the child opens his or her eyes.

Having lived without such fountain of knowledge
Is like crossing a long road between mountains
Without observing the colorful trees and flowery branches,
Missing the fundamental of life substance.
Your wife has served.
Offer the love your woman deserves!

Romantic Poems

Awake the Dream

I know you must be tired.
Lie down and relax.
First, put on comfortable attire.
Let me massage your neck,
Your shoulders, and lower back.
Listen to the silence and relax.
Take intense breaths and dream deeply.
Concentrate on my hands, moving with the flow of your breathing.
Let the dream be real.
Let it take you to the culmination with appeal.
Rise up serenely, and perceive the pleasing feelings.

Fame

The famous moments of essence
When the perfect boiling point is reached,
The cells collectively agree
To a grandiose festive encounter, indeed.
Like when the fall of a torrential rain upon an area ensues,
Soaks every particle it touches,
The fame of thrill is achieved,
And harmony revealed.

Sweet Stay

Let me sweeten your stay while I have you close in that style.
Let's be all the span of time aroused.
Your taste is of honey without textile,
To assimilate the reality of pleasure that is abound.

Let space narrow while you are present tonight
And time lengthen whilst our span contracts in desires,
Engaging the transition of time, when day becomes night;
Of what might become of the dark when the moon's light transpires?

In contemplating deliberate experiences in harmony:
What a beautiful night has it been,
Revealing so much energy in the morning,
The feelings that nature reveals through human beings.

Your Eyes

Your eyes are attractive with passion,
Are beautiful, encompass calmness;
Bring about desires and closeness.
They reveal love and compassion.

Wanting to inquire about your life story!
With obsession influenced by your personality,
With expectation of discovering that you are happy,
Desiring to share moments within your surrounding glory.

Can we take a walk in the woods outside of distractions?
To converse of the beauty of nature,
Allowing the human instincts to disperse into pleasure.
Trees and colorful leaves would be our major themes of attraction.

Poems of Friendship

The Beauty within Your Lips

The beauty carried in your skin
Reflects the one that I'm seeing.
Carry on with your smile,
And you will turn one on me
Certainly for a while.

You walk like a dancer,
Full of movements and elegance,
With a charismatic disposition,
A provocative energizer,
And a charming composition.

It is a blessing to smile.
Let it run with your natural and free style.
That's why nature made them brilliantly pure white,
So that they can be shown in total plenitude,
While enjoying natural truth and making everything bright.

Reasons to Smile

Why offer a warm hello to an unexpected
fellow?
It may not be a common occurrence, but easy
to follow.
It would improve both of their moods.
It would cause both to grin in salute.

What purpose of being,
Without sufficient beams?
Which reasons for existence should be pursued?
Not to be construed—a courteous hello with
a taboo.

What can a smile bring for humanity to
uncover?
It could be surprising, and a new experience
discovered.
During an unexpected encounter,
A soothing moment could be conquered.

With a grin inspired
And permanently, not admired,
An opportunity might have been lost,
Of moments presented to share, but the mind
is aloft.

A smile to somebody,
Including little buddies,
Arouses enthusiasms
Like the national anthem.

As water poured on grass that enhances growth,
Makes the surface greener on earth,
Extends life to all,
And creates loving souls.

A smiling face shows acceptance of others.
What most appropriate chance offered to one
another
To demonstrate what needs to expand
In this complicated world that we have in our
hands.

To reach a milestone, a most simple solution—
Is to take the first step and offer a smile as
option,
To show we are one in all.
It's a modest invitation to connect our souls.

Sparkling Smile

The girl who can run miles
Is attractive and courteous.
Is down to earth with a sparkling smile.

Carries herself elegantly with posture.
Loves life and treats people candidly
And venerates her family with passion.

Her smile demonstrates appreciation
And shows charisma.
Her smile reflects compassion.

A smile that emanates from the bodily soul cannot be explained,
Solely can be experienced and is much worthwhile.
A genuine smile is like the stars emitting sparks without constraint
In all directions, exhibited by an authentic sparkling smile.

Inspirational Poems

Be Happy

Jump out of bed without regret.
Do the routine you usually beget.
Look into the mirror and fix yourself.
Get ready with enthusiasm
Without meditating the transaction.

Travel where you need to get.
Admiring everything where your eyes are set.
Relish the varieties of the approaching sceneries—
The color and shape of trees,
To enjoy for free.

Don't look behind.
Thank God that you are not blind.
As you travel to the place that contributes
To your family to feed,
Please be an optimist, since you can see.

Beautiful All Over

The beauty within you has no limits.

It swells as you turn into yourself without restrictions

And get more attractive as the confidence level increases.

Don't look around for comparison.

Instead look inside yourself for uniqueness and keep going.

You will notice how everything in you will just keep growing.

Beauty has many definitions, always.

Do not concentrate on a general meaning.

Look for the beauty inside you first.

Please do not stop until you find it hence.

You will know when it happens.

It will be evident since you will start noticing your external magnificence.

Then there will be no stopping point.

Your internal and external splendors will just keep growing, or else!

They both will meet at the pinnacle on unison and emerge into one beautiful self.

Then there are no restrictions or control to your limits.

Your confidence will reach level of freedoms.

Will take you to the pedestal of unpredictable moments,

Reachable only by the influence of your confidence.

You will disclose to yourself, "I love myself and I."

Others will see your beauty and soul through the windows of your eyes,

Which expose truth and never lie!

Then peace establishes and happiness is present without neglects.

Accompanying you forever in this loving life.

You have brought the world into you rather than losing your internal energy to external perplexes.

Happiness

How can you be happy? Believing makes one so in substance.
When one gives, one will also receive per nature's justice.
Those who offer happiness abound
Are replenished in abundance.

Life pays back by doing good deeds.
Not in valuation but in emotional creation and potentiality, indeed.
To a stranger, verbalize words of sympathy,
Humble, simplistic jests of surprises and empathy.

Be cordial to everybody.
Demonstrate acceptance as you do to your buddies
With the opening of your soul
And friendly facial gestures to all.

Show your relaxation
Without restricted convention,
Depicting we are one and the same
Without separation of boundaries or disdain.

Appreciate the world and love nature
With all the people embraced.
Relax, and expect compliments of smiles and laughs.
Love life, and life will love you back.

Living

I love the day since I appreciate the blue sky.
I like the dark. Thus, I love the night.
I enjoy the shape of trees as I walk by.
I love life and relish the daylight.
I get lost in the clouds as I drive my car
And brake to a passing butterfly,
To increase its odds to survive.
I'm alive with love and gracefully enjoy life.

Young Mind

Hello, dear child, you represent the morning light,
Infused of energy engulfed by the sun,
An inspiration of hope refreshed in delight.
Follow the motivational instincts found in your mind,
Implanted by mother and father
To take you to places undefined,
Exerting moments unpredictable so far
That symbolize experiences solely enjoyable by hearts.

Your Mind

The spirit abounds in your mind.
Let it move freely around.
Fill the mind with clever substance
To value its significance.

The content of the spirit refills itself with abundance of happiness.
Observe as the mind overflows with peacefulness.
There is no available room for unwarranted elements' entry
Since it's all occupied with tranquility.

Enjoy in silence the beauty of nature,
Imagining the landscape of treasures
With attractive green grass and beautiful space.
It's an eye-catching view with flowery surface.

Look around, allowing your vision to traverse from tree to tree
As you enjoy their shapes and beautiful leaves.
Your spirit is at peace,
Provided by your mind with serenity which relish to be free.

Poems of Nature

Art of Nature

I built my house on the peak of a hill.
All sides surrounded by trees and flower bunches.
Every morning is like having a dream that I will observe the sunrise,
As the blooming gaze of the star rests upon the branches,
Creating the enlightenment of the paradise.

Standing outside on the elevated deck of the house,
In the distance, the sun transpires on the colorful trees for hours.
Every sunrise is a new occasion to enjoy the fabulous rays;
The variety of shapes portrayed by the contrast of poppy flowers,
Revealing a majestic rainbow of the colorful display.

Inspired by the glorious view,
Enlarges the extension of life endowed.
The happiness ensued in my heart,
Full of appreciation without doubt,
Can certainly be conquered by the elements of nature's art!

Clouds

Let's eat outside in the bright light beneath
The sun to enjoy the cool breeze,
Listening to the windy, bracing sound of the leaves,
As they wave toward the east.

Let's admire the white clouds
And observe as they freely move about drawing toys
As an airplane approaches making sound aloud,
Creating images for us to enjoy.

I can see in the upper center sketches of cows.
Look at the elephant's image in the upper west.
Birds gliding by the clouds,
And a tiger's figure with awkward legs.

Let's converse under the sun's rays,
Appreciating the warm light caressing
Our hearts to make us feel okay
While the subjects overhead, we continue addressing.

Why not enjoy the amazing fresh air?
Observing the blue sky over the mountain east,
Feeling the coolness as it traverses our hair,
And reflecting, how these sceneries fulfill us with peace.

The Gardener

The lady next door, with empathy,
Observes through her windows my art of gardening with sympathy.
The strokes in the ground intensify with energy deeper
To plant gardenia flowers with much interest.

The stance of each plant
Reveals characteristics according to its shape and brand.
Depicts a story with its presence and tone
With engraved history of its existence as a painting contains its own.

The story is subject to interpretation,
Unique to its beholder's mental creation.
It represents life's fundamental,
An illustration of human nature.

Sit back and relax.
You are the creator and director with tact.
Envision true beauty mature,
And contemplate the picturesque of beautiful Mother Nature.

In the Open

Relish eating outside in the open
To enjoy nature whilst your body gets healthy.
Disperse your vision around in distraction while hoping
Through the view of nature,
To admire observing birds as they fly and perch.
Listen to them as they sing and play,
Enjoying their frenzy movements and colorful display.

Concentrate on the combined sound of branches and creatures
To dissipate human automation
And bring life back to humane nature
Whereby we are supposed to reconnect,
Oftentimes to contemplate in circumspect,
To be constantly aware of the innate purpose
Of what living is meant to be—everything naturally exposed.

Lake Lanier

On Lake Lanier's man-made white beach,
The children play in the water, which is crystalline and rich.
They run and grab each other's feet, screaming and laughing, having a feast.

The parents relaxingly watch, sitting in the sand,
All the enjoyment caused by the daughters and son.
It's more captivating because the grandparents are part of the gang.

The elderly sit in beach reclining chairs,
Chatting with the son and daughter-in-law
While absorbing and enjoying the fresh, cool air.

The sky is bright blue, and birds are flying.
People are walking, and passing close by
With bunches of boys and girls admiring the flocks of bird glide.

Life in Circle

Standing on the apex of the mountain
Can see the top of the trees in the west side.
They appear small from my stance.
Do not measure importance by relative size,
But by the essence it provides.

You may pick up a drying leaf under a tree.
Should contemplate what it supplies,
As in conglomeration with others of its kind, would agree—
To sustain the survival of life
As it increases our wisdom of nature as a guide.

They contribute oxygen for our existence.
The dry leaves will resurface to life
Into substance for life path's continuance.
For they may convert into dirt and transform worms into butterflies
For us to admire them fly in the amazing cycles of life.

The Present

Here and now I exist,
Enjoying the beauty of the horizon.
This view will never exist again,
For it is unique in beauty, time, and space.
Thus, I immensely appreciate its presence,
For this unique experience brings life to my time
And its existence brings peace to my life.
Thanks, horizon, for the happiness you create in the present.

Raindrops Running

In the final days of summer, I jogged in the neighborhood.
Wanted to inspect the area since I didn't have a clue.
While climbing a steep hill, my breath wants to give up.
My persistence is not complacent. Certainly, I won't stop.

A clouded Sunday morning motivated the run
And insisted, not stopping till my resistance was gone.
Finally reached the top with the tank almost empty.
The relief was welcomed by my entire entity.

Jogging, I continued, after conquering the hill
And slowed the pace to keep myself instilled.
My lungs were relieved by a pleasant fresh air.
This place is attractive. I'm very well aware.

It's my new neighborhood, which I wanted to inspect,
Crisscrossing corners to appreciate the prospect.
The front yards are kept as if a party is gathering.
With such impressive landscapes, I wonder, "The owners must be gardeners."

Raindrops wet my arms, and I felt like an eagle, ready to take flight.
I wasn't expecting this prize, to fall from the sky.
Now I'm energized to complete the jogging task,
And sustained the trotting, witnessing the stunning facades.

The vicinity is packed with colorful crape myrtles.
It's a charming display of red, pink, and purple.
Is like a magical spell right in front of my face.
In this breathtaking neighborhood, I feel I won a race.

Red Wine

Do you wish to enjoy a refreshing glass of wine outside?
Exposed to nature in the open sky!
Meditating deeply with pride,
Touching earth with your toes and observing up high!
To be the object connecting the world to the blue sight!

Exposed to the refreshing wind on this shining day,
There you are, tasting the dark grapey wine.
Mesmerized by the pleasure of existence with faith.
Captivated as you survey the coastline.
Constricting the immense distance of space into your mind.

Searching for landmarks, you catch a different sight,

Worth envisioning in the distance,
Creating embellishing attractive sites
Of historical significance,
Preserving indelible marks entrenched in your life with relevance.

With a sip of wine, conceptualizing your existence,
You recapitulate and observe
With pleasantry and divine experience
That brings peace into your life,
With exclamation bearing approval of surprise.

Expressing essential appeals of harmony,
Desiring to share the radiant effervescence with your loved one,
You step into your home,
Demanding your man or woman
To share an additional glass of wine.

Scenery of Beauty

I am a tree high on a hill, overlooking beautiful sceneries.
I feel special, belonging to this magnificent space.
My leaves enjoy fresh air, exclusive to this area covered in greenery.
Proud to be terrestrial and part of this place.

In the morning, as the sun brightens the hemisphere,
I salute the rising sun with my stance.
With the levels of trees in the surrounding sphere,
And fish traversing the water's streams, I have the best view at any glance.

The sun's rays are reflected in the lake and plants,
In the mountain ranges and the rocks,
In the sky and planets,
Depicting the sky and clouds to be revealed as a giant photograph.

I thought I was beautiful but have concluded solemnly
That the expansion of water with its romances,
That the sky with the splendor of the sun daily,
The hills with the trees and peripheral branches,
Altogether form the perfect landscape in any version
To be admired and enjoyed by every person!

Special Life

Let the mountains be mountains!
To display different level of branches
With streams of water traveling under trees and caves
To gather to celebrate in a cascade.

Let the sky be the sky!
For scientists to observe past midnights
To discover the corners of the universe in a hurry
For us to span our minds with their extreme discoveries.

Let humans be humans!
With their special characters and unique personalities of man.
Let them span their brains
To experience the infinite sky with discovery of the minds,
To relish the mountain's display over the cascades.
And enjoy the human existence given to each of us for many decades.

The Stars

We see dim lights in the distant sky.
They are stars illuminating the other side.
In the far distance, the stars keep our mind mystified
And uphold us intrigued worldwide.

They appear by millions, giving us semblance of light.
Are kept afar not to interfere with the night.
As it's important for us to manifest,
They grant human the space to rest.

Stars exist by trillions in the distant heavenly.
Stay away by millions of miles, and increasingly
They amuse humans in the seven continents;
And are examined by scientists with cognizance.

The stars safeguard our intimate secrets for eternity.
We step outside to meditate with the infinity.
They are our counselors by decrees
And we admire them through windows with affinity to Christmas trees.

People in despair calm down in silence, contemplating the superstars.
Some in love advocate they rise to the stars.
Those in sadness share tears, and the stars shed serenity till the night cast out.
Content folks share their sentiments, exultingly all throughout.

Go outside to contemplate the night's fair.
Share passions of your life with the stars as you stare.
They will emit profound light with glares.
You will evoke abundance of shared emotions passed on from your forebears.

Twilight

The twilight reveals the contrast of day and night.
The stars that shine most when the moon is not so bright
Enchant with delight the surrounding earth
And fill us with emblems of faith.

In the twilight of our zone of hallmarks
When the tone of light turns into dark
Offers the opportunity to rest and romanticize
So that tomorrow we begin anew energized.

The fair of stars disappears out of view.
The startling sun is approaching you,
Embeds the stellar, all within its light,
And the sun converts the darkness into a spectacle of bright sight.

Poems of Encouragement

Absolute

Energized with persistence!
I'm continuing my struggles
Till my last breath of existence.
Don't look back at the trails,
For there is no mental return
That fit in the eternal trend.

Life is what you want it to be,
Which is never late to convey.
Depending how you perceive
Life in retrospect, moments casted away,
Determined to dissipate and disregard;
Anxious to correct slipups and recapture safeguards.

To kick stones out of the way,
Since you have more interesting objectives to follow
And better stages in life to reach your pathway,
Disregard minute concerns that are hollow.
Will harvest fruits with relevance in this planet
To the seeds you have in advance planted.

Without limits, every life is unique.
Do not equate your life to the rest of the pool.
Everyone has distinct and special characteristics.
Concentrate on your own aims and be cool.
Your dependents are the substance of your lifetime goals with much hope.
Learn from historical contexts, but apply your own scope.

Child and Father

A child asks his father:

What should I look for in life?
Look far into the distance.
It may be close or far.
Do not mind the instance.
You can go wherever your instincts will flare
As long as you are persistent
And have the wishes to explore.

Where should I start?
Look at the sky.
You can be one of those stars.
It is readily available for anyone to fly.
It seems to be unreachable but your inspiration becomes the anchor.
The blue sky is a reflection of life.
You can touch the celestial with your mind to conquer.

When can I begin?
Life is timeless, and you can begin whenever you please.
The sooner it happens, the more energy into space you will release.
The earlier you begin, the faster you will realize your dream.
History venerates successor dreamers who keep vivid the gleam.

Why should I do it?
You would improve yourself and the world.
Other people would benefit forever as well.
They will learn from your improvements and your errors.
Will build upon your accomplishments, and life altogether gets better.

Never Mind

Never mind the little things,
For they rob life of your existence.
Quickly think of something else, that brings
Peace to your mind and consistency.

Insist on a change of thinking … now!
For little things could be persistent
In trying to take possession of your rational,
When you dissipate and forget that you are resilient.

Don't ever take anything for granted.
You can always have the command
To dominate the little things unwanted
That you should never mind.

Pathway to History

A moment on earth called life!
Dedicated to the triumph that could exist,
Should be realized during one's existence
While conquering solemn peace.

Exploring the roads to happily evolve,
Forging, methodically the trajectory to manifest
With the persistence in life to focus upon one's goals.
Get to the end that would encounter the rhythm of peace!
To reach the pathway of life's centerpiece and syntheses.

Self-Powered

Incensed by transitions of life!
Thinking of positions to come!
Embarking in propositions posed by different outcomes!
Pondering on the chances poised to renounce!
But then again, why not push ahead with overwhelming force
To resist opposition persisting to hold one down,
Imposed by self-psychology that could be stronger than aspirations
To accomplish results bigger than oneself
With dignity full of inspirations?

Nothing or nobody can stop the vast and irresistible force
When it is produced from the inside of the self!

You Can

Proficiency does not come but through cultivated perseverance.
If you are feeling disheartened, remember you are not alone.
Most human go through a period of distress.
Don't forget, it will pass nonetheless.
The sooner the better to release the stress.

Think of a role model you admire.
Imitate that person mentally.
Be cool, but a persistent modeler.
Take the attitude of an unrelenting mule
And the stance of an indestructible tree.
Step with your feet on the negative ideas, pounding upon them,
And squash them with the weight of your body.
Crush those worries against the floor.
Disintegrate them out of existence
To a world called "Disappearance."

Come back to the real you with calmness, serenity, and coolness.

Think of the person you want to be
With self-assurance and the confidence of your role model.
Whether he/she is a family member, a friend, or whoever,
You can, if you think you can,
Become the person you want to be.
Everything you need to conquer is in your mind.
As long as you believe in yourself that you can, you will.

Hope and peace could be just one thought away.
Look for it most of the time deep within yourself and get it.
Consume yourself in the thoughts:
I trust myself.
I trust God.
I trust nature.
I love everybody.
I allow everybody to love me.

Other Poems

The Emblem of Truth

Truth is the authenticity of life
And promotes trust all around as well concerning your wife.
Its opposite engenders inaccuracy and alters nature under the sky
To an extent unpredictable by the author of a lie.

If aware of a negative rumor, like a double-edged knife,
That might affect someone's life,
Keep the gossip to yourself, even if it's hard,
Rather than revealing a conjecture that might break somebody's heart.

Everyone has suppositions, but not entitled to pass opinions as facts and fly,
For it might be insignificant in your eyes
But to parties of interest, it may cause destruction of lives. It's better to enhance nature
By individual personal assessment and measure.

If aware of a gossip of a loved one,
Allow the accused party acknowledges the charges at once
Before your judgment freely run
And regrettably create a pretentious outcome.

Do not allow the tale to grow and affirm on its own
When there is no merit of its certainty at front.
Everyone should get the chance to confirm or deny the accuracy of a sentence
Before a verdict destroys the ordinary livelihood and results in repentance.

Strong opinions travel through the unconscious.
Please don't allow illegitimate tales to mature in the subconscious
When fostered by unsupported proof
And sustain vividly the emblem of truth.

Insolence

Insolence is an ignorant intention, unmanaged,
Residing quietly inside, unchallenged,
Which won't be rectified without meaningful desire
To put off its fire.

During uncontrolled reactions,
One must address his actions.
How to conduct oneself with diplomacy
When it comes to prejudging others emotionally.

Acting self-centered with arrogance
Causes us all disadvantages
To believe having power to act
Without measures of the facts.

Expecting harmful behaviors then
Transpired by incidents
Place one in the worst stance
With no gain to sustain.

Who can live by himself?
To be true to the self
With courageous honor to demonstrate,
Show kindness, not arrogance that isolate

To benefit your culture in all respects
And to live in sublime harmony, show your inherent intellect
With inspirational patience to others,
The same affection one exhibits to his sisters, brothers, and mother.

Precepts

Emphasize self-trust.
One of the best qualities to have.
Everything will be built on that thrust.
Anything discouraging won't affect your guts.

No matter what, be fearless.
First, be unafraid in your mind.
Everything begins in the world of your brain cells.
You can conquer whatever you entertain of any kind.

Believe you can, and you will
Portray a life of promise.
You can get to your infinity with goodwill.
You can be whole and accomplished.

Do not ever give up. Be persistent.
Your blood is continually pumping up.

Resemble the internal body, a constant system.
Be vibrant—the body likes that.

Improve every one of your qualities.
The foundation of humankind ought to be challenged.
Be an inspiration of intent novelties.
Let your spirit fly with the freedom of knowledge.

Regardless of your accomplishments, be humble.
Emphasize self-trust.
No matter what, be fearless.
Believe you can, and you will.
Do not ever give up. Be persistent.
Improve every one of your qualities continually.
And always be a person of all the people.

Life Rekindled

From an individual's perspective, can life be rekindled? It depends on each person's belief and conviction. As the old saying goes, "You can, if you think you can." When you have a problem and that crisis is holding you down, you can define your life by that dilemma. You are as small or as big as the problem itself. You can be measured by it. It is the rock or mountain blocking the passage. It controls your survival and your life. While the problem persists in the mind, it represents your best goal. It is improbable that you can improve yourself or contribute to the betterment of others while your soul is involved in an unproductive pursuit. Get out of it fast so that you may start to live and begin appreciating the harmony of living, and allow love and passion to dominate your existence. Unconsciously and automatically, the benefit will be passed onto other relatives or friends in the process. Life is too short to be wasted. Just look in retrospect and observe how sudden the passage of time is or could be.

Farewell

My intent is to write poems with passion about the beautiful exposures and experiences of life. Nature has so much to offer that we ought to describe our experiences so other people can read about them since, as individuals, we can only cover so much and the encounters should be shared. It is imperative to remain receptive to enjoy the simplicity presented by life and the wonders offered by nature. When we have conviction about life, ideas will flow effortlessly and as naturally as a free breeze endows the space in our surroundings. The passion of life is to be enjoyed every second of ours days. Let the palpitations of your heart remind you of that.

Do not contrast life to material value; rather, enjoy the pleasure of the occasion and the gratification of life. Emphasize the historical moments of joy, and disregard the unkind instances that do not deserve to be underlined. Proclaim happiness through your breathing while aspiring to triumph by the peacefulness you have inspired in others. Declare the beauty of the mountains, the trees, and the smiles depicted by the plants through the flowers, those that we so much admire. Announce silently how their beauty subtly enhances our lives. How the love that we feel is a reflection of nature itself. Let's share with one another at any scale the beauty we all may exert or have, to enrich our world of which common sympathy and courtesy are quite noteworthy.

On a different note, I would love to hear from you. Do not think twice; your opinions and suggestions are welcomed. Please e-mail me at angelpoetry28@gmail.com.

My regards.